Party Rental Business Playbook

By J.H. Dies

A Newbiz Playbook Publication

J. Hilton Dies retains the exclusive rights to any use and training applications of the Party Rental Business Playbook. Copyright© 2016 by newbizplaybook.com All rights reserved. Printed in the United States of America. No part of this book may be used or reproduced in any manner whatsoever without written permission except in the case of brief quotations embodied in critical articles and reviews. For information address Newbiz Playbook Publishers at **products@newbizplaybook.com**

FIRST EDITION

For downloadable tools emailed directly to you please email **products@newbizplaybook.com** use the password moonwalkbizpro in the re: of the email

For my family, the answer to my why

Understanding Your "Product"

The fundamental truth about the party rental business is that the product is, for those who hire you, fun. Parents and the families who call you are looking for you to bring joy to their homes. The experience is the product. You and your staff need to be on time or early, professionally dressed (suitable for the situation i.e. a nice logo collared shirt and jeans or nice shorts is fine for delivery guys), and friendly.

If you take excellent care of people, your referral network can grow, and you can build a premium brand. Little details like a birthday card for the kid involved, or an extra flavor of snow cone syrup will add to the experience and value your clients receive inexpensively, while allowing you to command a premium price.

Nordstrom's is not an inexpensive store. Their products are expensive, even more expensive than other stores by a fair margin, but their client service and return policies are exceptional. The Ritz Carlton hosts very nice facilities, but honestly for the cost, they are not materially better than many less expensive hotels. The difference is in service, and the way they make their patrons feel.

Ignore this fundamental truth, and none of these contents will matter. Embrace it, and you will succeed. The goal is to create Raving Fans at every opportunity. The clients you help will have friends and family hosting parties, and you want them to insist on you to handle them.

Customer Rental Agreement

REPLACE WITH YOUR LOGO HERE

This contract is made and entered into this__day of__ 2016 by and between the undersigned Lessee, and [YOUR COMPANY HERE], hereafter known as the Lessor and is mutually agreed that the contract shall be subject to the information in this contract.

PARTIES: The Lessee hereby engages Lessor who agrees to furnish the items described upon the terms and conditions set forth herein.

DEPOSIT: A deposit of $ shall be delivered to and in the name of [YOUR COMPANY HERE], upon signing of this contract. The items mentioned in this contract are not reserved for the Lessee until this deposit is received. This deposit is not refundable unless the rental cancellation is received 10 days prior to the rental.

BALANCE: The remaining balance of $ is due upon arrival at the event.

TIMING AND FEES: The reserved rentals shall be delivered no later than 15 minutes before the requested start time unless both parties agree upon other arrangements.

The equipment should be empty of riders at the requested end time. An additional hour will be charged if the pickup agent must wait for the equipment to be vacated.

SETUP AND OPERATION: The Lessee should have at least 1 person of average strength per inflatable available to assist with setup at the time of delivery, if needed. This person should be the person who will be responsible for operation of the ride. Lessee is responsible for enforcing posted rules. Instructions for safety and operation will be reviewed at the time of setup.

<u>AT NO TIME SHOULD THE EQUIPMENT BE LEFT UNATTENDED!</u>

SPECIAL PROVISIONS: The Lessor reserves the right not to perform outdoor engagements when, in the Lessor's judgment, weather conditions would be detrimental to the Lessor's equipment. This includes but is not limited to wind, rain, or mud. A suitable indoor location should be reserved as an alternative site in the event of poor weather conditions.

<u>*A representative from the Lessor will contact the Lessee prior to delivering the equipment if the weather is questionable. Once the equipment arrives at the event, the deposit is not refundable. At the time of this call, if the Lessee chooses not to have the equipment delivered due to weather concerns, the full deposit will be returned.</u>

NEGLIGENCE OR ABUSE: Lessee agrees to be responsible for any damage to Hullaballoo Rentals equipment, if damage is incurred while the equipment is in the possession of the Lessee. Damage fees vary but are estimated below:

Bounces: $50-$100 for cleaning fees
               $200-$500 for repairs
               $3500 if the unit is not repairable

No food, drinks, animals, shoes, or sharp objects are allowed in the rentals at any time. The operator is responsible for ensuring that the size and weight of persons entering the inflatable does not exceed the maximum. Rentals that are set up on hard surfaces such as concrete or asphalt must be closely watched to prevent their moving. If the equipment moves off the provided tarp, damage or staining may occur on the bottom of the unit.

If the Lessee chooses to deflate the equipment prior to the arrival of the pick-up attendant, it must be re-inflated before it is packed up. The unit will be inspected and receive a preliminary cleaning before removal.

The Lessee expressly assumes the responsibility of informing all person(s) who use, operate or rent the above specified rental equipment that, they do so at their own risk and that, if any injury occurs to the person(s) using, operating or renting the equipment, [YOUR COMPANY HERE], it's employees, officers, directors, shareholders, agents, successors and assigns shall not be held liable for any such injuries and/or resulting damages and, further, shall indemnify [YOUR COMPANY HERE] in the event they are held liable for any injuries and/or resulting damage.

This contract contains the entire agreement between the parties and shall not be enlarged or modified except in writing and signed by all appropriated parties.

Please note that in the event of an emergency or problems with equipment, it is up to the Lessee to contract The Lessor at YOUR NUMBER HERE immediately in order to expedite the problem. If Lessee fails to contact us, the Lessor is not responsible for any refunds

HOLD HARMLESS PROVISION- LESSEE AGREES TO INDEMNIFY AND HOLD LESSOR HARMLESS FROM ANY AND ALL CLAIMS, ACTIONS, SUITS, PROCEEDING COSTS, EXPENSES , DAMAGES AND LIABILITIES INCLUDING REAASONABLE ATTORNEY'S FEES ARISING BY REASON OF INJURY, DAMAGE OR DEATH TO PERSONS OR PROPERTY, IN CONNECTION WITH OR RESULTING FROM THE USE OF THE EQUIPMENT INCLUDING BUT NOT LIMITED TO, THE MANUFACTURE, SELECTION, DELIVERY, POSSESSION, USE, OPERATION, OR RETURN OF THE EQUIPMENT INCLUDING BUT NOT LIMITED TO THE EQUIPMENT. LESSEE HEREBY RELEASES AND HOLDS HARMLESS LESSOR FROM INJURIES OR DAMAGES INCURRED AS A RESULT OF THE USE OF SAID EQUIPMENT UNLESS LESSOR IS OPERATING THE EQUIPMENT AND IS DEMMED BY A COURT OF LAW TO BE NEGLIGENT IN IT'S ACTIONS. LESSOR CANNOT UNDER ANY CIRCUMSTANCES BE HELD LIABLE FOR INJURIES AS A RESULT OF ACTS OF GOD, NATURE, OR OTHER CONDITIONS BEYOUND ITS CONTROL OR KNOWLEDGE.

DUTY TO MITIGATE- IN THE EVENT OF INJURY, DAMAGE OR LOSS DUE TO LESSOR'S NEGLIGENCE, LESSEE AGREES AND ASSUMES THE DUTY TO MITIGATE ALL COSTS RESULTING FROM SAID INJURY, DAMAGE OR LOSS.

DISCLAIMER OF CONSEQUENTIAL DAMAGES- BY SIGNING THIS CONTRACT, LESSEE AGREES TO FOREGO SEEKING ANY CONSEQUENTIAL DAMAGES IN THE EVENT OF ANY INJURY DAMAGE OR LOSS DUE TO LESSOR'S NEGLIGENCE.

DISCLAIMER OF WARRANTIES- LESSOR MAKES NO WARRANTIES EITHER EXPRESSED OR IMPLIED AS TO THE CONDITION OR PERFORMANCE OF ANY EQUIPMENT AND/OR PROPERTY LEASED BY LESSEE FROM LESSOR. BY SIGNING THIS CONTRACT, LESSEE AGREES THAT ANY WARRANTY OF MERCHANTABILITY OR FITNESS OF A PARTICULAR PURPOSE ARE HEREBY DISCLAIMED BY SIGNING THIS CONTRACT, LESSEE AGREES THAT NO EXPRESS WARRANTY AS TO THE CONDITION OR PERFORMANCE OF ANY EQUIPMENT AND/OR PROPERTY LEASED BY LESSEE IS HEREBY DISCLAIMED.

MERGER CLAUSE- THIS SIGNED CONTRACT INCOMPASSES THE ENTIRE AGREEMENT BETWEEN THE LESSOR AND THE LESSEE. NO AMENDMENT, WHEATHER FROM PREVIOUS OR SUBSEQUENT NEGOTIATIONS BETWEEN THE LESSEE AND THE LESSOR, SHALL BE VALID OR ENFORCEABLE UNLESS IN WRITING AND SIGNED BY ALL PARTIES TO THIS CONTRACT. THE INVALIDITY OR UNENFORCEABLEILITY OF ANY PARTICULAR PROVISION OF THIS AGREEMENT SHALL NOT EFFECT THE OTHER PROVISIONS HEREOF.

_____
Lessee Signature

Date of Event: **Phone Number:**

Lessee:

Address of Event:

Setup Time: **End Time**:

Reservation Details:

Choosing your Inflatables

Obviously, you are purchasing inflatables! It's time to determine the size, style, and prices of the units you are going to purchase.

Size:

Usually, you can't go wrong if you start out with **13x13**'s. One person can handle them, they fit in most driveways or yards, and are big enough for festivals and larger events.

If your target market lives mostly in cluster homes with small yards, you may prefer a **10x10**. These will not be as versatile as the larger size but if they suit your target market, it makes more sense to start with the smaller units. They are also easier to handle. If you think you may have trouble handling the inflatables and plan to do the setup yourself, a smaller unit is the way to go.

The **15 x 15** size moonwalk is extremely versatile. It is heavier than the 13 x13 but can still be handled by one person. Small enough to fit in most yards but big enough to handle enough children for festivals and large events, the 15 x 15 is a good choice if you are only purchasing one bounce to begin.

If you live in a colder climate, you may want to consider a **Garage or Indoor Bounce**. These are smaller and lower to the ground so that they can fit in a garage. The 10 x 10 size fits in almost any small space, including some living rooms! The 10 x 13 and 10 x 15 sizes are designed to fit perfectly in

1/2 of a 2-car garage- leaving room for the party in the other half of the garage. The Indoor Bounce has multiple uses- great for rainy days and winter time, it also functions as a mini bouncy-boxing ring or a party bounce for young children all summer long. It makes an excellent addition to your regular bounces, giving you the ability to adapt to weather and other unusual setup conditions. At least one Indoor Moonwalk is highly recommended for all moonwalk rental businesses.

Style:

How do you choose from so many styles available? It's hard to go wrong on a style unless you get something extremely specific that goes out of style next year. Classic styles such as the castle or fun house or birthday cake are best if you are only starting out with one unit. You don't want something to "boyish" or "girly" if you only have one or two units.

Buy more specific characters as your business expands. Of course, if you really want a certain character, go for it!

Another idea is to ask a "focus group" which one they would like best. Ask kids and moms and daycare workers which one they would want. But make your own decision- if you have 50 choices, you are likely to get 50 answers!

Other Equipment

Trailer:

Yes, you can fit a single bounce in the back of a truck or van to start out. Your life will be much easier if you get a trailer if you can afford it. A 5'x8' trailer can handle 2 or 3 15'x15' bounces and is a good choice for your new business. A trailer will make loading, unloading and possibly even storage easier for you.

Dolly/Handtruck:

Don't buy the cheapest handtruck you can find. You will need a commercial quality handtruck with inflatable tires. The tires are important because the inflatable kind are wider and have better traction for moving heavy equipment over lawns and gravel. The hard rubber type of tires are more likely to tear up lawns and cause you to have to struggle to get the equipment where you want it.

We highly recommend the Inflatable Mongo Mover, a hand truck specially designed for moving inflatable rides. The fenders prevent the wheels from rubbing the vinyl and the specially angled wheels take the strain off your back. A Mongo Mover is a MUST if you are buying a slide or other heavy piece of equipment.

If a Mongo Mover is out of your price range, try buying a hand truck designed for moving appliances. They come with straps conveniently attached and are designed for heavy loads.

Sandbags and Sandbag Covers:

Follow your manufacturer's instructions on stabilizing your equipment. You will need sandbags for hard surfaces and the easiest way to connect sandbags is with sandbag covers. The minimum you will need is 4, with one on each corner. We recommend you use 8 sandbags per bounce, with 2 on each corner. It is a small price to pay in extra covers and a little extra effort when you consider how much an insurance claim may cost you in the long run. You can usually purchase sandbag covers from your manufacturer at the time you buy your equipment or you can buy them separately later.

If you don't have sandbag covers, you can purchase duffel bags and place your sandbags inside. Secure the handle to your tiedown rope. Remember, nylon duffel bags will not last as long as vinyl sandbag covers and will need to be replaced sooner.

Tarps:

If your manufacturer does not include a tarp with your equipment purchase, you will need to purchase one. It is not a bad idea to go ahead and purchase backups as well. A tarp is very inexpensive in comparison to your equipment and you should always use one, whether you are setting up on grass or concrete. Buy the highest quality tarp you can get, whether locally or through your manufacturer. It goes a long way towards protecting your investment. We recommend you ALWAYS use a tarp- then there is no question as to whether or not you should use one for a specific setup.

On potentially rainy days, it is a good idea to leave an extra tarp with the client and ask them to deflate the ride and cover it with the tarp in the event that it starts raining. If the rain then stops, they can re-inflate the ride with no worries. If it is pouring down rain, the tarp won't help- you are still going to have to deal with a wet, heavy unit!

Stakes:

Stakes will be used to secure your equipment on grass. Follow your manufacturer's instructions. You will need lightweight tent spikes for securing the tarp and heavy duty stakes for securing the inflatable. We recommend that you purchase landscape spikes at your local home improvement warehouse for about .30-.50 each and find washers to fit. Get a heavy hammer or a mallet to pound them into the ground. If you use a hammer, you can use the claw end to pull the stake out later or you can purchase a claw-type tool to help you remove the stakes.

While 4 spikes are adequate, we recommend that you use 8 spikes per unit with 2 stakes on each corner secured to rope loops for maximum stability. Always follow your manufacturer's recommendations on securing your unit and check to see if your insurance company has any specific requirements as well.

Extension Cords:

Purchase heavy-duty outdoor type extension cords. A good idea is to purchase one with a small LED light on the end so that you can tell if there is a problem with the power source. The ones that have a locking mechanism are great for added safety against the cord pulling out. One 50' cord per unit should be enough; you really don't want to extend the power any farther than 50'. It is a good idea to have a longer one just in case you need it, though.

Generator:

If you live in an area where you know you are going to be setting up a lot in areas with no power, look into costs for gas generators. As a rule of thumb, start out renting a generator when you need one until you can determine how often it will be needed and what size you will need to purchase. It is a good idea to call around and get rental rates so that you will have answers on hand when a customer asks. Plan your pricing accordingly.

Carpet Remnant:

This is a great idea. Place a large carpet remnant in front of the moonwalk, under the safety step. This gives kids a place to sit and put their shoes and it minimizes grass and dirt that get tracked into your equipment. Definitely worth the effort because it will save you a lot of time cleaning.

Cordless Vacuum:

Buy the most powerful cordless hand vac you can find, one with a hose and a crevice tool. This will help you quickly clear the moonwalk of any grass or debris before you deflate and roll it up.

Broom and Cleaning Supplies:

A smaller broom with an angled head is better than a bigger one since you are dealing with lots of crevices in the moonwalk floor. Spray Lysol and a small towel will help you to quickly clean any spots before they become permanent.

Stopwatch

A stopwatch is a nice touch to offer your clients. They can play timed games with it or time turns if there are a lot of children at the event. If you are attending the rental, you will want a stopwatch to ensure that the length of the turns are fair.

Whistle

If you are attending an event, take a whistle to get the attention of the riders. You don't know their names and often there is a lot of noise to overcome. This is really a safety issue as you will often need to get the attention of a rider who is misbehaving before an accident happens.

Wind Gauge

Inflatable rides should not be operated in winds that exceed 25 MPH so it doesn't hurt to have a wind gauge on hand to help you or your customers make that call. These run about $125-$150 in camping/sporting goods stores. Nice to have but not essential.

Liability Protection For Your Party Rental Business

The following section will address liability protection for your business. Given the excitement of the children playing, the dynamic nature of the activity, and other factors, you must be prepared first to do what you can to avoid injuries and accidents, and if they happen, you want to be in a position to protect your business.

Even with the liability protections we have included, you cannot guarantee that there will be no accidents, or that someone will not sue you for injuries sustained using your equipment. We can however, help you to protect your business as well as possible from having to pay large sums to those involved in an accident.

Preventative Measures

Your company should print safety signs that travel with your rental equipment with all of the rules for using that equipment. The sign should have your name and logo, as well as the rules associated with safe use of the equipment, such as number of kids allowed, etc.

Some equipment comes with Velcro patches and signs with safety rules written by the manufacturer. Make sure these are clean legible, and attached at all times.

Insurance will be discussed in great detail below, but it is important, and in most cases a requirement of the law, that your business be insured with a policy that covers damages associated with injuries sustained while using your equipment.

As soon as practical, your business should be registered as an LLC, or S corporation. Most states have an easy to use form on their websites, to allow for the creation of these entities. This

will protect your personal assets from being attacked in the event of a legal dispute.

The customer rental agreement must be signed by all of your customers, prior to installation of equipment. If the client refuses to assign it, do not complete the delivery. Most insurance requires that you use a liability protection agreement such as the one in this book. In many cases, even if there is an injury, no one will even call you to report it, as they will know they have signed a waiver of liability. This agreement also protects you against damage done to the units, or theft, while you are not in possession of the unit.

Insist that your clients supervise the units if you are not leaving an attendant there to do that to make sure children are using them safely. It is also a good idea to teach the clients the basics of operation of the equipment to save a trip if a breaker is blown, or a kid unplugs a power chord by accident.

The Importance of Insurance

I have spoken to a number of party rental business owners, especially those just starting out, who are debating whether or not they need insurance. My experience is a little bit unusual in that, my business is a joint venture with a friend, but I am a practicing attorney in Texas. Here are a few insurance realities:

•   Insurance for this industry is very expensive relative to the revenue generated, especially when just starting out;

•   Insurance is required by a number of desirable customers, such as those who are hosting their functions at parks, or on public property, and schools and churches, who often rent multiple units;

•   In many states, such as Texas, insurance is a requirement of the business. You can and will be fined if the state discovers that you do not have insurance;

•   If your business is a sole proprietorship, as opposed to a corporation or llc, you can be personally liable to customers in the event of a lawsuit that doesn't go your way;

•   Most insurance is going to require you to document the units you have available for rent, and many carriers want to see the customer rental agreement you have with customers. If you need one of these, see moonwalkbizpro.com, or other vendors selling business software and forms.

It can be frustrating to spend such a large percentage of your incoming revenue on coverage, but without it, one claim could be devastating to your company. Certain customers will never be viable prospects, and the state could even shut your business down. Therefore, you have to treat insurance like any other business expense, such as lights, delivery, or employees. Put

away a piece of your rentals early in the year, and it won't feel so painful, when you have to spend money on a large insurance premium.

As far as finding cost effective insurance, I would recommend that you have your agent shop several different carriers 90 days or more before your renewal. I have seen swings in premium of up to a thousand dollars, for similar coverages with the same policy terms, and coverage limits. It's certainly worth your time.

Also, you must be scrupulously honest with your insurance carrier. If you provide any inaccurate or dishonest information, a carrier could use that as a basis to deny coverage when you need it most. Make sure your agent has the facts straight, and when you add or sell units, make sure your carrier knows. Finally, in the event of a claim, advise the carrier immediately, don't talk to the customer about whose fault it is until you have spoken with counsel, since doing so could void your coverage! Or worse, you could admit fault for something that is not legally your fault. Delaying in reporting the claim, or taking action which increases the exposure to the insurance company could reduce, or void important coverage terms you paid so much money for.

While I am an attorney, this blog is not intended to be used or treated as legal advice. I am in Texas, and the laws of your jurisdiction or area could be different. As always be sure to speak to counsel immediately if you or your business get sued.

Insurance is like so many other things. It's better to have it and not need it, than need it and not have it.

Insurance Contacts

Below are some insurance contacts in various parts of the country that offer or have offered coverages for this business. Also reach out to your own personal insurance agent to see if they have options as well.

Britton-Gallagher & Associates
www.insureair.com
Toll Free: (866) 703-4777
Fax: (440) 544-1234

Sihle Insurance Group
Phone: 800-728-0988
Fax: 407-774-0936

The Adams Company
225 Columbia Ave.
Lexington SC 29072
Phone: 803-359-4108

The Insurance Depot
Cape Coral FL
Phone: 239-543-7473

Gilmore Insurance & Associates
Phone: 704-788-1415

Waterford Insurance
(800) 284-6687

Szerlip Insurance
(201) 467-0400

National Sports Rec. Association
Greenville, SC
Ph. (864) 297-9727
www.nsera.com

Neil Oliver Insurance
Ph: (770) 478-6548
www.inflatableinsurance.com
(AL, GA, TN, SC)

DeSanctis Insurance
Ph: (781) 935-8480 x50
www.desanctisins.com

Dick Wardle Insurance Brokers
Ph: (800) 298-3000
www.wardlowinsurance.com

Friedman Group, Inc.
Ph: (563) 556-0272
www.friedman-group.com
(MN, IA, WI, IL, MI, IN)

Evolution Insurance Brokers
Ph: (800) 321-1493
www.eibdirect.com
(All states)

Allied Insurance
(814) 764-5523

Mendel Kaliff Insurance
San Antonio, (210) 829-7634

Allied Specialty Insurance
Treasure Island, FL
(800) 237-3355
www.alliedspecialty.com

Haas & Wilkerson
Shawnee Mission, KS
(800) 821-7703
www.hwins.com

Beckman Insurance
(414) 497-8160

Acordia of WV
Charleston WV 25326
Phone: 304-347-0748
Phone: 800-922-9244

Specialty Insurance
Tom Plouffe
Phone: 203-927-4280

JBL Trinity West Insurance
Edmond, OK
(405) 216-8118

Cossio Insurance Agency
Simpsonville, SC
Ph: 864-688-0121
www.weinsureinflatables.com
(All states)

Promt Insurance
Newport Beach, CA
(949)646-8684
Refer to Policy XJJ Inflatables
(CA only)

Altemeier-Oliver & Co.
Cincinnati, OH
Ph: (513) 984-5335
www.aoc-insurance.com
(All states)

JT Lake Insurance Services
Ph: (916) 338-3277
(CA, IN, WS, IL, IA)

Cole Humphrey
Ph: (419) 634-8010
(Ohio only)

Mulvey Insurance Agency, Inc.
Ph: (866) 856-7070
(FL, MI, NC, NJ, NY,OH PA,TN,WV)

Isner Insurance
Ph: (614) 236-8691 x107
www.isnerinsurance.com
(IL, MI, MD, NY, OH, PA, WV)

Saint Pauls Insurance
(800) 241-9245

Scottsdale Insurance
Scottsdale, AZ 85258
(480) 948-0505

Inglis Insurance Brokers
San Francisco, CA
(800) 532-6917
www.inglisinsurance.com

Cornerstone Insurance
Anaheim, CA
(714) 490-0500

Sihle Insurance Group
Altamonte Springs, FL
(800) 298-3000

Altemeier-Oliver Co.
9902 Carver Rd. Ste. 200
Cincinnati, OH 45202
Ph: (513) 984-5335
Fax: (513) 984-5445
www.aoc-insurance.com

Cossio Insurance Agency
107 Old Laurens Rd
Simpsonville, SC 29681
Ph: 864-688-0121
Fax: 864-688-0138
www.weinsureinflatables.com

DeSanctis Insurance
Ph :(781) 935-8480
Fax: (781) 933-5645
www.desanctisins.com

Dick Wardlow Insurance Brokers
Ph: (800) 298-3000
Fax: (805) 553-0404
www.wardlowinsurance.com

Evolution Insurance Brokers
Ph: (800) 321-1493
Fax: (801) 304-3733
www.eibdirect.com

Event Planners Association
(866)380-3372 Phone
(866) 230-3044 Fax
www.eventplannersassociation.com

The Friedman Group Inc.
880 Locust Street – Suite 200
Dubuque, IA 52001
Phone: 877-580-7066
**http://www.friedman-
group.com/productsservices/specialty.html**

National Sports Ent.
Association
155 Verdin Rd.
Greenville, SC 29607
Ph. (864) 297-9727
Fax (803) 753-9797
www.nsera.com

Neil Oliver Insurance
Ph: (770) 478-6548
Fax: (770) 477-7033
www.inflatableinsurance.com

Accordia
www.acordia.com
Acordia of WV
One Hillcrest Drive E (25311)
P.O. Box 1551
Charleston WV 25326 Phone: 304-347-0748
Phone: 800-922-9244
Fax: 304-347-8483

Adams Company
225 Columbia Ave.
Lexington SC 29072 Phone: 803-359-4108

Allied Specialty Insurance
www.alliedspecialty.com
1045 Gulf Blvd.
Treasure Island FL 33706 Phone: 800-237-3355

Altemeier Oliver & Company
www.aoc-ins.com
ONLY WRITES IN: Ohio-Kentucky-Indiana
9902 Carver Rd., Ste. 200
Cincinnati, OH 45202 Ph: 513-984-5335
Fax: 513-984-5445

Beckman Insurance
Phone: 414-497-8160

Byrne Risk Management
Phone: 949-230-3195

Cole Humphrey
ONLY WRITES IN: Ohio
P.O. Box 263
Ada, OH 45810 Phone: 419-634-8010
Fax: 419-634-2245

Cornerstone Insurance
Phone: 714-490-0500

Cossio Insurance Company
www.cossioinsurance.com
107 Old Laurens Rd.
Simpsonville SC 29681 Phone: 864-862-2838
Fax: 864-688-0138

Cross Roads Ins.
Jason Collins Phone: 336-996-7788
Fax: 336-996-7785

DeSantis Insurance
www.desantisins.com
WRITE ONLY IN: East Coast
  Phone: 781-935-8480

Diversified Insurance
2 Hamill Road Suite 155
Baltimore MD 21210 Phone: 410-433-3000
Fax: 410-433-3440

Evolution Insurance Brokers
www.eibdirect.com
WRITES IN: ALL 50 States
 Phone: 800-321-1493
Fax: 801-304-3733

First Commercial Insurance
WRITES IN: Florida Only
Tony Cannizzaro
Jacksonville, FL Phone: 386-775-1781

Freidman Insurance Group
www.friedman-group.com
Writes In: AL, AR, AZ, CO, FL, GA, IA, IL, IN, KS, KY, LA, MI, MN, MO, MS, NE, NC, NV, OH, OK, OR, PA, SC, TN, TX, VA, WA, WV, WI
Contact: Sandi Swift Phone 877-580-7066 ext 234

Gilmore Insurance & Associates
 Phone: 704-788-1415

Golden State West Insurance
www.goldenstatewest.com
WRITES IN: California Only.
 Phone: 916-830-1042

Haas & Wilkerson
www.hwins.com
P. O. Box 2946
Shawnee Mission, KS 66201-1346 Phone: 800-821-7703

Inflatable Industry Purchasing Group
http://iiins.csiprotection.com/
John Carr Toll free (888) 411-4911

Fax (678) 832-4910

Inglis Insurance Brokers
www.inglisinsurance.com
P. O. Box 24522
San Francisco, CA 94124 Phone: 800-532-6917
Fax: 800-567-0354

International Specialty Events Insurance
Jim Quist Phone: 800-521-1709
Fax: 801-304-3735

Isner Insurance
Don Pirtle
221 S. Hamilton Road.
Columbus OH 43213 Phone: 614-236-8691
Fax: 614-961-3408

JBL Trinity West Insurance
P.O. Box 7284
Edmund OK 73083 Phone: 405-216-8118
Fax: 405-216-8228

JT Lake Insurance
Phone: 916-338-3277
Fax: 916-338-3622

Lawson & Blevins
WRITES IN: California Only.
Phone: 800-760-0433

Mendel S. Kaliff Waterford Insurance
1250 N.E. Loop 410 Ste. 920
San Antonio, TX 78209 Phone: 210-829-7634
Fax: 210-829-7636

Mulvey Insurance Agency Inc.
www.mulveyinsurance.com
WRITES IN: FL MI NC NJ NY OH PA TN WV
Phone: 866-856-7070
Fax: 330-856-2255

Neil Oliver Insurance
WRITES IN: GA, AL, SC, TN
Phone: 770-478 6548
Fax: 770-477-7033

Saint Pauls Insurance
Phone: 800-241-9245

Scottsdale Insurance
8877 N. Gainey Center Dr.
Scottsdale, AZ 85258 Phone: 480-948-0505

Sihle Insurance Group
P.O. Box 160398
Altamonte Springs FL 32716 Phone: 800-728-0988
Fax: 407-774-0936

Specialty Insurance
Tom Plouffe Phone: 203-927-4280

Company Name
Company Address
Company Phone #

INCIDENT & ACCIDENT REPORT

Insured's Information

Name of Insured:_____

Contact
Name:_____

Phone number and best time to contact: _____AM

Policy Number:_____

Effective Date of Policy:_____

Description of Injured Party

Name of Injured Party:_____

If a minor, legal guardian's name:_____

Address:_____

_____

Employer:_____

Home Phone: ( )_____

Business Phone: ( )_____

Description of Accident

Date of Injury:_____

Time of Injury:_____

Activity Participating In:_____

Describe in detail how the accident happened (use back of paper if necessary):

_____

_____

_____

_____

_____

_____

Describe the injured party's mental status at the time of the accident:

☐ Confused ☐ Calm ☐ Panicked ☐ Aggressive ☐ Other:_____

Describe environment/ general atmosphere around incident:

_____

_____

_____

_____

Describe location of the site where the accident occurred:

_____
_____
_____
_____

Describe the weather (if outdoors):

_____
_____

Temperature (estimate if necessary):_____°F

Did equipment contribute in any way to the accident?

☐ Yes ☐ No

If yes, please describe:

_____
_____

Did the Injured Party contribute to the accident in any way?

Yes ☐ No

If yes, please describe:

_____

_____

Did the Injured Party state that he or she contributed to the accident in any way? ☐ Yes ☐ No
If yes, please describe:

_____

_____

_____

Did another participant contribute to the injury? ☐ Yes ☐ No

If yes, please describe:

_____

_____

_____

Were an photographs taken? ☐ Yes ☐ No

If yes, please enclose all photographs.

Activity time lost: ☐ None ☐ ½ Day or More ☐ Ended Participation

Describe an First Aid given (include a list of any medications given):

_____

_____

_____

Did the Injured Party refuse first aid or evacuation? ☐ Yes ☐ No
If yes, please describe:

_____

_____

_____

_____

Does the injured Party take any medication or have any allergies?
☐ Yes ☐ No
If yes, please describe:

_____

_____

_____

_____

Is this a re-injury of an old condition? ☐ Yes ☐ No

Person (s) supervising the rental unit on site at the time of accident?

Name   Age   Experience

_____   _____

_____   _____

_____   _____

_____   _____

PAGE 3
Has the injured Party been at this location before? ☐ Yes ☐ No
If yes, please describe:

_____

_____

_____

Does the injured Party currently have medical insurance? ☐ Yes ☐ No
If yes, with what company:

Name of Company_____

Policy #_____

PERSON COMPLETING THIS STATEMENT:

SIGNATURE_____

DATE_____

PRINT
NAME_____

ADDRESS_____

_____

PHONE_____

Witness Statement of Accident or Incident

STATEMENT OF ACCIDENT

The use of this form is to obtain statements pertaining to the accident's occurrence, and to obtain information on future accident prevention.
Please answer each question to the best of your ability.
Thank you for helping us with this matter.

PLEASE PRINT

1. Describe events leading up to the accident.

_____

_____

_____

_____

_____

_____

2. What happened?

_____

_____

_____

_____

_____

3. Describe what happened after the accident took place.

4. Can you think of any way this type of accident could have been avoided in the future?

5. Were sufficient warnings, instructions, and information provided?

Name of person making statement:_____

Address:_____

Phone:_____

Signature:_____

Date:_____

Managing Your Inventory

Inflatable Unit Delivery Checklist

- [ ] Inflatable Unit
- [ ] Blower
- [ ] 2 50' Extension Cords
- [ ] 8 Small Tarp Stakes w/ washers
- [ ] 8 Large Unit Stakes w/ washers
- [ ] Tarp
- [ ] Hand Truck
- [ ] Carpet Remnant

Optional:

- [ ] Stopwatch
- [ ] Whistle
- [ ] Wind Gauge

Paperwork:

- [ ] Map to Event Address
- [ ] Rental Agreement   Copy
- [ ] Operating Instructions

Cleaning Supplies:

- [ ] Broom
- [ ] Vacuum
- [ ] Cleaning Spray
- [ ] Towel
- [ ] Broom
- [ ] Disinfecting Cleaner

Choosing your Inflatables

Obviously, you are purchasing inflatables! It's time to determine the size, style, and prices of the units you are going to purchase.

Size:

Usually, you can't go wrong if you start out with **13x13**'s. One person can handle them, they fit in most driveways or yards, and are big enough for festivals and larger events.

If your target market lives mostly in cluster homes with small yards, you may prefer a **10x10**. These will not be as versatile as the larger size but if they suit your target market, it makes more sense to start with the smaller units. They are also easier to handle. If you think you may have trouble handling the inflatables and plan to do the setup yourself, a smaller unit is the way to go.

The **15 x 15** size moonwalk is extremely versatile. It is heavier than the 13 x13 but can still be handled by one person. Small enough to fit in most yards but big enough to handle enough children for festivals and large events, the 15 x 15 is a good choice if you are only purchasing one bounce to begin.

We recommend starting with a brightly neutral colored unit that can hold Velcro banners customized to fit the theme of the party. Ninja jump made a very popular unit that allowed for Disney themed characters, and others to be changed out with such banners. It was discontinued because the versatility of the unit reduced the number purchased. It is always risky to start with themed units. Kids are very selective about what they want at their parties, and neutral units are fine. As your business grows, you can add the favorites like princesses for girls, etc., but that is not where you should start.

Combo units, or those units with a bounce house and slide are very popular and allow for a larger number of kids to flow in and out, making them better for larger parties. Start neutral and expand to themed units as your business grows.

If you live in a colder climate, you may want to consider a **Garage or Indoor Bounce**. These are smaller and lower to the ground so that they can fit in a garage. The 10 x 10 size fits in almost any small space, including some living rooms! The 10 x 13 and 10 x 15 sizes are designed to fit perfectly in 1/2 of a 2-car garage- leaving room for the party in the other half of the garage. The Indoor Bounce has multiple uses- great for rainy days and winter time, it also functions as a mini bouncy-boxing ring or a party bounce for young children all summer long. It makes an excellent addition to your regular bounces, giving you the ability to adapt to weather and other unusual setup conditions. At least one Indoor Moonwalk is highly recommended for all moonwalk rental businesses.

In warmer climates waterslides, and water sprinkle units are very popular, and command higher rental prices.

Style:

How do you choose from so many styles available? It's hard to go wrong on a style unless you get something extremely specific that goes out of style next year. Classic styles such as the castle or fun house or birthday cake are best if you are only starting out with one unit. You don't want something to "boyish" or "girly" if you only have one or two units.

Buy more specific characters as your business expands. Of course, if you really want a certain character, go for it!
Another idea is to ask a "focus group" which one they would like best. Ask kids and moms and daycare workers which one they would want. But make your own decision- if you have 50 choices, you are likely to get 50 answers!

Other Equipment

Trailer:
Yes, you can fit a single bounce in the back of a truck or van to start out. Your life will be much easier if you get a trailer if you can afford it. A 5'x8' trailer can handle 2 or 3 15'x15' bounces and is a good choice for your new business. A trailer will make loading, unloading and possibly even storage easier for you.

Dolly/Handtruck:
Don't buy the cheapest handtruck you can find. You will need a commercial quality handtruck with inflatable tires. The tires are important because the inflatable kind are wider and have better traction for moving heavy equipment over lawns and gravel. The hard rubber type of tires are more likely to tear up lawns and cause you to have to struggle to get the equipment where you want it.

We highly recommend the **Inflatable Mongo Mover**, a hand truck specially designed for moving inflatable rides. The fenders prevent the wheels from rubbing the vinyl and the specially angled wheels take the strain off your back. A Mongo Mover is a MUST if you are buying a slide or other heavy piece of equipment.

If a Mongo Mover is out of your price range, try buying a hand truck designed for moving appliances. They come with straps conveniently attached and are designed for heavy loads.

Sandbags and Sandbag Covers:
Follow your manufacturer's instructions on stabilizing your equipment. You will need sandbags for hard surfaces and the easiest way to connect sandbags is with sandbag covers. The minimum you will need is 4, with one on each corner. We recommend you use 8 sandbags per bounce, with 2 on each corner. It is a small price to pay in extra covers and a little extra effort when you consider how much an insurance claim may cost you in the long run. You can usually purchase sandbag covers from your manufacturer at the time you buy your equipment or you can buy them separately later.

If you don't have sandbag covers, you can purchase duffel bags and place your sandbags inside. Secure the handle to your tie down rope. Remember, nylon duffel bags will not last as long as vinyl sandbag covers and will need to be replaced sooner.

Tarps:
If your manufacturer does not include a tarp with your equipment purchase, you will need to purchase one. It is not a bad idea to go ahead and purchase backups as well. A tarp is very inexpensive in comparison to your equipment and you should always use one, whether you are setting up on grass or concrete. Buy the highest quality tarp you can get, whether locally or through your manufacturer. It goes a long way towards protecting your investment. We recommend you ALWAYS use a tarp- then there is no question as to whether or not you should use one for a specific setup.

On potentially rainy days, it is a good idea to leave an extra tarp with the client and ask them to deflate the ride and cover it with the tarp in the event that it starts raining. If the rain then stops, they can re-inflate the ride with no worries. If it is pouring down rain, the tarp won't help- you are still going to have to deal with a wet, heavy unit!

Stakes:
Stakes will be used to secure your equipment on grass. Follow your manufacturer's instructions. You will need lightweight tent spikes for securing the tarp and heavy duty stakes for securing the inflatable. We recommend that you purchase landscape spikes at your local home improvement warehouse for about .30-.50 each and find washers to fit. Get a heavy hammer or a mallet to pound them into the ground. If you use a hammer, you can use the claw end to pull the stake out later or you can purchase a claw-type tool to help you remove the stakes.

While 4 spikes are adequate, we recommend that you use 8 spikes per unit with 2 stakes on each corner secured to rope loops for maximum stability.

Extension Cords:
Purchase heavy-duty outdoor type extension cords. A good idea is to purchase one with a small LED light on the end so that you can tell if there is a problem with the power source. The ones that have a locking mechanism are great for added safety against the cord pulling out. One 50' cord per unit should be enough; you really don't want to extend the power any farther than 50'. It is a good idea to have a longer one just in case you need it, though.

Generator:
If you live in an area where you know you are going to be setting up a lot in areas with no power, look into costs for gas generators. As a rule of thumb, start out renting a generator when you need one until you can determine how often it will be needed and what size you will need to purchase. It is a good idea to call around and get rental rates so that you will have answers on hand when a customer asks. Plan your pricing accordingly.

Carpet Remnant:
This is a great idea. Place a large carpet remnant in front of the moonwalk, under the safety step. This gives kids a place to sit and put their shoes and it minimizes grass and dirt that get tracked into your equipment. Definitely worth the effort because it will save you a lot of time cleaning.

Cordless Vacuum:
Buy the most powerful cordless hand vac you can find, one with a hose and a crevice tool. This will help you quickly clear the moonwalk of any grass or debris before you deflate and roll it up.

Broom and Cleaning Supplies:
A smaller broom with an angled head is better than a bigger one since you are dealing with lots of crevices in the moonwalk floor. Spray Lysol and a small towel will help you to quickly clean any spots before they become permanent.

Stopwatch
A stopwatch is a nice touch to offer your clients. They can play timed games with it or time turns if there are a lot of children at the event. If you are attending the rental, you will want a stopwatch to ensure that the length of the turns are fair.

Whistle
If you are attending an event, take a whistle to get the attention of the riders. You don't know their names and often there is a lot of noise to overcome. This is really a safety issue as you will often need to get the attention of a rider who is misbehaving before an accident happens.

Wind Gauge
Inflatable rides should not be operated in winds that exceed 25 MPH so it doesn't hurt to have a wind gauge on hand to help you or your customers make that call. These run about $125-$150 in camping/sporting goods stores. Nice to have but not essential.

Bubble Machine
OK, so you don't NEED a **Bubble Machine**, but they are a lot of fun and add to the rental fees for almost no work. Don't forget to stock up on bubble solution!

Cleaning Wet Inflatables

The most discouraging part of the inflatable industry is RAIN! Properly drying inflatables is one of the most time consuming but required things we have to do to maintain our equipment. Some inflatables have the big access zippers were small people can actually climb in and vacuum / dry out the units. If you have these units, please do not go into them without someone around to help in case of an emergency.

Some operators say if it is a light rain, leave the units blown up, problem with that is the blower will suck in water to the unit. Deflating it will allow water to enter through the seams. Having the customer fold it and covering it is the best thing if there is no one available to roll it up.

When an inflatable is blown up the air pressure will hold water up against the vinyl and not allow all of it to blow out the seams. Some of the baffle material and netting will also absorb and hold moisture.

When I have wet units we blow them up and tilt them to one side (facing the sun) with a hand truck under it for support. This allows standing water to go to one side and blow out of the stitch work. When it appears dry from the outside remove the hand truck, deflate the unit and allow any water up in the columns and support tubes to run back down. After it is deflated, blow it back up again. This will allow water to move around and drain out again. We repeat this operation several times to allow it to dry completely. We also spray Microban into the unit which will kill and prevent mildew from starting.

In some worst cases where a unit has been left out in hours of rain we resort to slitting a small hole on the BOTTOM of the unit towards the front corner and tilt the unit on its side to allow water to flow out of it on site. This can be easily patched when you get it back and dried out.

By doing it in the same area for your units it will also make it easier if it happens again. Just pull the patch off the next time. It is on the bottom of the unit so looks are not all that important.
You will find that some manufactures use material that can hold up longer than others. I do set a priority though. Anything with digital graphics or clear vinyl gets cleaned first. The water seems to want to damage the graphics before plain or painted vinyl.

The most important thing is to get them dry ASAP. There is a substantial investment in this business and once mildew has set into the scrim of vinyl it is impossible to get out.

Ordering Units

We get a large number of questions about where to find inexpensive, quality, equipment. We have purchased equipment directly from the manufacturer, imported equipment from overseas, and we have purchased used equipment in great condition online from places like craigslist. Each of the approaches has strengths and weaknesses.

For example, we have purchased a great deal of equipment from craigslist. Be safe, and smart in how and when you approach anyone you do not know to purchase something expensive like this. Very often people purchase new equipment, and struggle with getting gigs, suffer an injury that makes it hard for them to handle the labor side, or get bored of the business. These folks can give you incredible deals on units if you are smart about how you buy. Insist that each unit be inflated. Leaks, hand patches, and obvious repairs are big warning signs and substantially reduce the value of the unit. Make sure that the unit is tight and firm to the touch when inflated. If seems have stretched from wear and tear, the unit will be hard if not impossible to repair, and will be less fun for those who use it. One drawback to this approach is that you may take trips to buy, only find out units do not meet your standards. This is the most economical way to purchase units, and you can get great deals on multiple unit purchases.

Importing. Inexpensive units can be obtained overseas from manufacturers in China, and elsewhere. Alibaba.com is a website that can put you in touch with different manufacturers. Always ask for American clients you can speak to about unit quality. Pay partial deposits, and insist on pictures of the constructed units, or ask to see them on skype to insure that they are progressing as you expected. Quality units can be obtained this way less expensively than purchase from local manufacturers. One drawback is the hassle of working with a customs broker, and the delivery delays associated with getting the units to you which can take an additional 30-60 days after the unit is completed. This does give you flexibility in unit selection and design.

Purchase from American manufacturers. There are a number of quality manufacturers, such as ninjajump and others that build units that will last a long time. These are expensive, and you are often limited to their availability and selection.

Party Rental Business Planning and Payment Forms

[Company Name]
[Company slogan]

[Street Address]
[City, ST ZIP Code]
Phone [Phone] | Fax [Fax]
[Email] | [Website]

TO
[Name]
[Company Name]
[Street Address]
[City, ST ZIP Code]
Phone [Phone] | [Email]

INVOICE

INVOICE # [Invoice No.]
DATE [Date]

FOR [Project or service description]
P.O. # [P.O. #]

Description	Amount
Total	

Make all checks payable to [Company Name].
Payment is due within 30 days.
If you have any questions concerning this invoice, contact [Name] | [Phone] | [Email]

THANK YOU FOR YOUR BUSINESS!

Competition Tracking Chart

Business Name	Address	Phone #	Equipment	Pricing	Extras

The idea behind the competition tracking chart is to do ongoing market research of competitors, their offerings, and their pricing to allow you to make decisions about such matters in your own business. Some competitors will have websites that tell you the availability for units in the coming weeks. A great idea is to look for units that are booked weeks out as potential add-ons for your own business.

We also recommend monitoring Craig's list for items for sale, and track them to your competition. A competitor may have made the decision to go out of business, and this is a good way to get insight into that, as well as a lead on potentially great buys for units to add to your business.

Client Tracking Chart

Tracking Client information is a great way to help with targeted marketing, and to identify those great customers who keep using your service. We use a simple excel spreadsheet and track the following:

Customer Name
Contact Person
Phone
Email
Address
Last Contacted
Last Ordered
Notes

Maintenance Report

Maintenance Report

Equipment	Size	Serial#	Purchase Date	Price	Vendor

Cleaned Date

Repair Date	Repair Description	Price	Vendor

To be able to command top price for your units in your area, they will need to be tracked for all cleaning, repairs, costs, and issues. This chart will help you spot trends in wear and tear, and maybe quality issues with manufacturers. It will also allow you to make smart decisions about rolling inventory out of the business to keep the newest and freshest equipment with your customers.

If an item does well, see if it is still being manufactured, and if so, purchase another one, and sell your older unit (you can get 60-80 percent of purchase value on units that are cleaned and maintained). We recommend rotating units roughly every two years with normal regular rentals. Units that are rented less often can be held longer.

Each unit should have its own maintenance report. This also shows regular maintenance and cleaning, which can help you command a better price in selling your used units.

Reservation Documentation

Rental Reservation

Client Name:
Phone:
Alt Phone:
E-mail:
Fax:
Today's Date:

Event Date:
Start Time:
End Time:
Est Delivery Time:
Est Pickup Time:

Equipment Reserved: Cost:

Delivery Fee:
TOTAL FEES:

Mailing Address:

Event Address:

Setup Surface:

Directions:

Special Requests:

Agreement Mail Date:
Deposit Received Date:
Deposit Amount:
Balance Paid Date:
Balance Amount:

NOTES:

Marketing for The Party Rental Business

Of all the challenges a new business owner faces, marketing the business can feel the most overwhelming. The good news is that you can very easily, and inexpensively market your business to a receptive target audience. The challenge will be follow through and consistency in maintaining exposure for your brand.

Whole books have been written on the subject of marketing, and this material is not designed to replace them. Our hope is to provide you with guidance as to how to spend your time, and where. You should understand the pros and cons of the various options out there, to make intelligent decisions on your ROI or return on investment. Everyone has different results with different media. As important as this is to your success, you should track where your leads (especially the ones that hire you), are coming from. Advertising that appears expensive at the outset, maybe cheap relative to other options when you see the revenue it is generating.

Website/SEO

Your website if properly done can be a very useful marketing tool, and may be one of the places you spend early money, once you start getting rentals. Wordpress.org, has some incredibly easy templated websites that can get you started. If you can get to a place where you are on the first or second page of google with your site, which is very doable, this will be the single most effective marketing vehicle you have. Keep in mind, you aren't looking to be first when someone types "bounce houses." You are looking to be first when someone type "party rentals in Cleveland." The difference between these two is what makes it vastly easier to rise to the top. I have, with no training whatsoever, been able to get several service based websites on the first page of google.

The key is to duplicate the search you want to be relevant for. For example, if the hope is that you come up first when someone types "moonwalk rentals in St. Louis," do that search, and then go to the sites on the first page and a half of google, and look at the content. You are specifically looking for whether there are videos or pictures, how often your key search term appears.

You are also looking for the titles used for the website's pages. For example if you click on a page, at the top right side of that page there will be a tab, with some language on it that is designed to summarize the content of that page. These are title tags, and this research on content, will tell you what you need to emulate to get to the top of google. Be careful. Copying text and directly duplicating material, or over using a few key words will get you punted from key word searches, which would kill the effectiveness of your website. When you start to book events, you should consider early investment in a great website with an SEO (search engine optimization) professional to help you.

We recommend that at a minimum, a third of all profits go back into the business to grow it and help with important investments in the business. This investment would be at the top of that list. If you have some resources already saved, this would boost visibility substantially and increase the speed with which your business gets noticed. There are a number of free-lance website development options out there. Do your research as this is a hugely important investment.

Networking and Word of Mouth

Experienced, successful rental companies will tell you that most of their new business comes from referrals and relationships they have formed with clients, day cares, schools, churches, parks and rec centers, and others in the business. When renting to a customer, I try to show them how what I have will meet their needs, but if they want a very particular unit I do not have, I would rather refer them to a reliable company and maybe get their business next time, then simply wish them good luck.

The challenge is to reach the level where the "machine" is sending you leads on a constant basis. As you build relationships with clients, schools, churches, and parks and rec centers, it is reasonable to expect that they will tell others about your business. You should be candid in hiring these folks about what you are looking for

In the beginning you should be very vocal to your personal network of friends and family to let them know you have begun to do this work, being sure to emphasize all of your efforts, research, and time spent getting to know the business.

Social Media

Social media is an incredibly effective and inexpensive means of advertising your business, and to a limited degree it is worth your time to learn how to get your brand up and running on Facebook, Instagram, twitter, Pinterest, and snapchat. This is how you build a following, and stay relevant to others who need to think of you first when they or someone they know decides to use your products or services. In the beginning these are free if not very inexpensive. Once you get traction, placing ads may make a huge difference. Next to website and SEO, this can be the most impactful marketing media available to you.

Ratings and specialty sites

There are a number of sites like Yelp, which allow businesses to put up very basic profiles for free. In the beginning, it can be helpful to put your site and business on as many of these as possible so that these sites point back to your website and business. When you sign up, you will be pitched on pay packages that help boost your chances of appearing early on these sites. In our experience these types of investment don't generate nearly as many live leads as search engine optimization. It is important to monitor these sites, and to regularly search for your site so that you can see what reviews are out there both good and bad, which could impact your business.

Phone books, mailers and other print advertising

We address these last, because frankly they are not very effective in generating revenue relative to the cost, at least in this business. At some point, you may be large enough to require a better add in a phone book, or need to have mail outs for clients to stay in front of them, but getting email addresses, and electronic communication is vastly more effective. We simply don't recommend spending startup dollars here.

You may have need for printed material in the form of business cards or trifolds, which can be handed out to guests who visit you at wedding shows etc. These are necessary expenditures, and when they are printed it should be high quality work on good card or paper stock. This stuff represents your brand, which must be elite if you want to command larger fees with your engagements.

We have included a great example of a tri fold in word form, so you don't have to play with formatting or make one yourself. Simply cut and paste photos or logos and add content as you see fit. Below is a printed example with two sides of a suggested layout, with content references that will allow you adjust the tri-fold to fit your business.

Tri Fold Template

To get started right away, just tap any placeholder text (such as this) and start typing to replace it with your own.

This would be a great place for a mission statement.

You can use this fresh, professional brochure just as it is or easily customize it

On the next page, we've added a few tips (like this one) to help you get started. To replace any tip text with your own, just tap it and begin typing.

Company Name
Street Address
City, ST ZIP

Recipient
Street Address
City, ST ZIP Code

replace with
LOGO

Website
Email

Tel Telephone
Fax Fax

Company Name

Products and Services

replace with
LOGO

Think a document that looks this good has to be difficult to format? Think again!

- To easily apply any text formatting you see in this document with just a tap, on the Home tab of the ribbon, check out Styles.
- Use styles to easily format your Word documents in no time. For example, this text uses the List Bullet style.

Find even more easy-to-use tools on the Insert tab, such as to add a hyperlink, insert a comment, or add automatic page numbering.

View and edit this document in Word on your computer, tablet, or phone. You can edit text, easily insert content such as pictures, shapes, and tables, and seamlessly save the document to the cloud from Word on your Windows, Mac, Android, or iOS device.

So what do you include in a brochure like this?

We know you could go on for hours about how great your business is. (And we don't blame you—you're amazing!)

But since you need to keep it short and sweet here, maybe try a summary of competitive benefits at left and a brief success story here in the middle.

The right side of this page is perfect for those glowing testimonials and a list of key products or services.

Don't be shy! Show them how fabulous you are.

"Your company is the greatest. I can't imagine anyone living without you."

—Very smart customer

"This style is named Quote but you can also use it to call attention to an important piece of info."

—Your friends in Word

What you offer:

- Product or service
- Product or service
- Product or service
- Product or service

Your most impressive clients:

- Big, important company
- Another really well-known company

Setting up a Moonwalk

Setting up a Moonwalk

Step 1: Check the Area and Setup Tarp

It is a good idea to get a duffel bag or work bag to hold your "stuff"; stakes, straps, extension cords, extra rope, tape, etc.

Check your site for stones, sticks, or other obstructions. Check for the nearest electrical outlet and TEST IT before you start. This can save you a lot of work later. Many outdoor outlets do not work. Once you have your site ready, unfold your tarp.

A word about tarps: some people do not use them on grass setups. We always use a tarp a) to protect our investment and b) so a driver isn't making the decision whether to use a tarp or not. The picture shows the tarp unfolded and ready to be staked down.

Stakes: Shown here are lightweight tent spikes used to hold the tarp in place and 18" landscape spikes with washers for securing the inflatable unit. You can use heavy-duty tent stakes for the inflatable unit as well. We like the landscape spikes because you can use a hammer or mallet to drive them securely into any type of soil, even hard-packed clay.

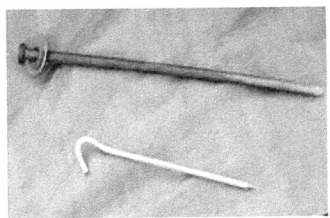

Stake down your tarp in at least 4 corners, driving the tent spike all the way into the ground so no one will trip on it. You may want to drive spikes into the center hole of each side of the tarp as well, although the corners are usually enough. It is important to stake down your tarp to prevent it from moving while you are setting up the inflatable unit.

Step 2: Unload the Inflatables

We show a trailer being used. Many people use the back of a van or a truck to deliver inflatables.

Unsecure the units.

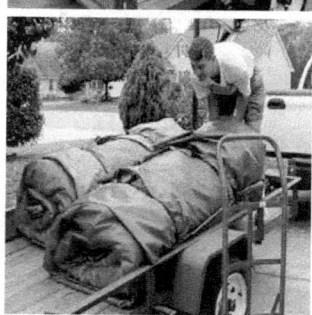

Tip the unit up on the rolled end.

Once the unit is on its' end, pull your hand truck into place. It is important to place the unit on the hand truck with the blower tubes facing out, on the opposite side from the hand truck. The tubes show you where the back of the unit is so that you know which side you need to place toward the blower. This will help you to easily position the unit on the tarp, ready to unroll.

Slide the hand truck under the unit, then tip it back onto the hand truck and roll it off the trailer. This hand truck has inflatable wheels- they are much better for this type of work than the hard-wheeled type of hand truck. Hard wheels tend to tear up grass and drag in low traction conditions.

Step 3: Setup

Good placement on the tarp will make unrolling easy.

Position the unit in the center of the back of the tarp (wherever you plan to place the blower). Tip the unit forward and pull the hand truck out from under it. Then allow it to fall back onto the tarp with the blower tubes on top.

You may need to adjust the unit to that it lines up correctly and is centered.

Unknot the straps and remove them. Place them in your bag so you don't lose them.

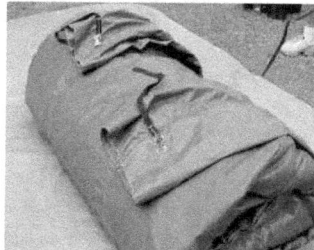

Unroll the blower tubes.

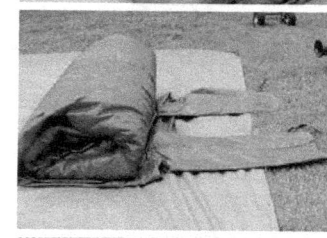

Unroll the unit.

Unfold the sides and straighten them out.

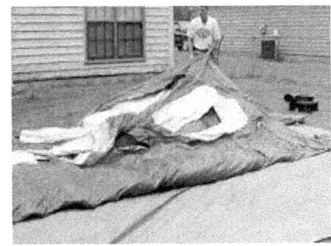

Step 4: Secure the Inflatable Unit

Securing the unit is a critical safety step. Check with your insurance company to see if they have any specific requirements for your state for how the unit must be secured.

We will demonstrate the double-tie-down method. In many places, you can use a single tie-down on each corner, but it only takes a few minutes to do two tie-downs. We have two heavy nylon rope loops about 2 1/2 feet long looped through our tie-down ring.

Pull the loop out at an angle from the unit. Make a small loop at the end of the rope loop and place the spike through it. Pound the stake into the ground at an angle away from the inflatable unit for best stability. The loop and washer keep the rope securely held to the stake.

Stake down the second tie-down at an angle to the first. The ropes should not be taut- there should be some slack to allow the unit to move a bit as it is being used. If you were using sandbags, you would attach the handles of the sandbag covers to the ropes with carabiners and place them at the same angles. Stake down each corner.

Step 5: Inflate & Inspect

Inflating only takes a minute or two! Don't skip a quick inspection before you allow the kids in.

Most units have two blower tubes on them. On the one that will not have the blower attached to it, you will need to close the opening. Pleat or fold the vinyl fabric as tight as you can, then use the attached strap to secure it shut. This doesn't have to be airtight- expect some air to leak out of this tube. Escaping air is what make your unit bouncy.

Hook the blower up to the other tube. Slide the blower opening into the tube, then pleat and fold the extra fabric around the blower to hold it while you tighten the strap. Wrap the strap around the blower and tube and tighten. Make sure you have gathered all the fabric in the strap, especially around the bottom, where it is hard to see. All set!

Check to make sure your extension cord is away from foot traffic as much as possible. Arrange the cord so that it is away from the entrance of the unit. Make sure all children are away from the unit before you turn the blower on. Simply plug in the blower and turn it on. Inflatation only takes a minute or two. Kids will want to get in immediately but make sure you complete your inspection and training with the responsible party first.

Take off your shoes and get in the unit with spray cleaner, a rag, and a small vacuum. Quickly check for anything that may have been missed in the last take-down cleaning. Then walk around the unit and inspect it for any dirt or damage. You may want to have the responsible person (if you are leaving it unattended) walk with you. Then review operating instructions and emergency procedures with the responsible party before packing up and heading out.

Setting Your Prices for Moonwalk Rentals

Pricing Your Services

Pricing your rental service is a tough decision, especially when you are just starting out. How much should you charge? The answer is "as much as the market will bear".

Rentals are different across the country. The length of the season and number of competitors are big factors in what you can charge for your rental.
Competition

The first place to start is a competitive analysis. Hopefully, you did this before you placed your order for inflatables, but if not, get to it now!
Call your competitors, check out their websites, and keep your eyes open for advertisements and flyers in your area. When you call, make sure to find out:

- How they structure the timeframe for their rentals
- What the prices are
- Whether that price includes delivery and tax
- How much of a deposit they require (if they do)
- What type of payments they accept
- The size, quantity and condition of their units

It feels a little funny at first, but trust me, they will be doing the same to you soon enough! (Remember when calling that many people have caller)

Write all the information out in a spreadsheet or even on paper; it will make it easier to compare prices and services.
Differentiation

Now it's time to think about what makes your business different.

Your rental period may be different, your service better, your inflatables newer. Why do you need to know this stuff to set your pricing? Because it makes a difference! When potential clients call you, you want to be able to be confident when you quote a price that your service is worth it. Thinking through all the variables prepares you to "sell" a client on the value of hiring you.

Pricing

Low Cost Leader

You may think that the best way to start out is by undercutting all of the competition. This is not the way to go for most companies.

I do recommend this strategy to people who are buying older equipment and don't want to put a lot of time and energy into building the business. There are plenty of people out there looking only at costs and there will be business for the lowest-cost company in the area.

What I have found is that people shopping on the basis of cost are also the ones most likely to abuse or neglect your equipment and they also complain the loudest, wanting discounts for setup delays, rain, or any other little thing they can find to complain out. If this doesn't bother you, than low-cost is the strategy for you.

Introductory Prices

This is the strategy I recommend to most startup companies. Don't start out with low prices- go ahead and price your rentals at a fair price. You need business to get started, so offer introductory specials to stimulate business.

The advantages of this strategy are:

- You get people to take a chance on you, an unknown company

- You establish the price in their mind so they aren't surprised when they call you next year
- You don't erode the "going rate" for rentals in your area, forcing other companies to lower their prices to compete
- You influence their decision with the idea of getting a "bargain"; a better service/equipment for a good price
- You have the opportunity to convince customers that you do a good job and they will recommend you to others

High/Low Prices

The high/low strategy is very similar to the introductory pricing, except that you maintain lower prices through changing promotions.

Many companies will use this strategy during slow periods (such as the winter) and other times they need to stimulate business. The main benefit to high/low pricing is raising the value of a rental in the mind of the customer and helping them to feel smart by hiring you because they are getting such a good deal.

Premium Pricing

Premium pricing should be the goal of every rental company. You want your services to be in such demand, that you can charge a profitable fee and still stay busy. Less work, more money!

This strategy is ideal for companies who focus on clean, well-maintained equipment and top-notch service for their deliveries. It's not just an ideal, it really works. By building customer loyalty over a period of time, you can get such glowing referrals that your clients wouldn't dream of calling anyone else or shopping around.

What Works for You?

Every rental company needs to carefully consider their pricing strategy when starting out. While it's easy to lower prices, it is very difficult to raise them. Try to stay within a reasonable range for pricing in your area so that you don't set an expectation that moonwalk rentals are a cheap commodity or an expensive indulgence.

MOCK INCOME ANALYSIS:

INITIAL EXPENSES

$_____ Inflatables (Prices Vary greatly)

$_____ Concession Machines

$_____ Games

$_____ Sandbags ($7 - $10 each)

$_____ Stakes ($5.00 each)

$_____ Hammer (Free - $5.00)

$_____ Safety Cones ($5.00 each)

$_____ Bucket (Free - $5.00)

$_____ Roll of duct tape ($3.00)

$_____ Hand Truck (TH-800 mentioned previously is $90.00)

$_____ Trailer (price varies greatly)

$_____ Buying a domain ($8.95 - $35.00 shop around)

$_____ Having Website Built (Free - $250.00)

$_____ Becoming and LLC or a Corp (varies greatly $150 - $300, contact a local attorney or state department)

$_____ Business Licenses (States vary: may require state, county and city licensing.)

$_____ Printing of Liability Contract and Safety Waiver (depends on quantity required and how many carbonless copy forms you may want/require).

$_____ Vacuum (do you want a cordless/rechargeable?, prices vary greatly)

$_____ Misc. / Unknown / Unexpected Expenses

WEEKLY EXPENSES

$_____Fuel

$_____Labor

$_____Cleaning Supplies

$_____Labor for Cleaning

$_____ Misc. / Unknown / Unexpected Expenses

MONTHLY EXPENSES

$_____Website Hosting ($5.00 - $10.00)

$_____Phone

$_____Yellow page ad

$_____Other advertising

$_____ Flyers

$_____ Business Cards

$_____Car/Truck Magnets or vinyl graphics

$_____ Newspaper

$_____ Radio Stations

$_____ Local children's magazines

$_____ Misc. / Unknown / Unexpected Expenses

YEARLY EXPENSES

$_____ General Liability Insurance ($550 - $1200 PER unit, varies greatly)

$_____ Income taxes

$_____ Business Insurance

$_____ Business License (reapply yearly)

$_____ LLC or Corp reports (Meeting minutes must be sent to your appropriate state department yearly. You may have to have an attorney prepare yearly paperwork)

$_____ Equipment Replacement

$_____ Misc. / Unknown / Unexpected Expenses

$_____ YEARLY ESTIMATED GROSS INCOME

$_____ GROSS INCOME – ESTIMATED EXPENSES = (net income)

$ _____ NET INCOME

$ _____ Divide by Hours spent taking reservations, cleaning and delivering.

$ _____ Equals your Hourly Wage

www.ingramcontent.com/pod-product-compliance
Lightning Source LLC
Chambersburg PA
CBHW070719210526
45170CB00021B/834